Fantastic Creatures

Andrew Whitmore

sundance
A Haights Cross Communications Company

a black dog book

Published by Sundance Publishing
P.O. Box 1326, 234 Taylor Street, Littleton, MA 01460
800-343-8204

Copyright © text Black Dog Productions

First published 1999 as Phenomena by
Horwitz Martin
A Division of Horwitz Publications Pty Ltd
55 Chandos St., St. Leonards NSW 2065 Australia

Exclusive United States Distribution: Sundance Publishing

ISBN 0-7608-8035-2

Printed in Canada

Contents

Author's Note

I've been a big fan of myths and legends all of my life. Perhaps I never quite grew up. I enjoy reading about dragons, giants, and snake-haired monsters. That's one of the reasons I write fantasy and science fiction stories. This lets me create as many wild and fantastic creatures as I like.

It's almost as much fun trying to discover the truth behind these tales. Sometimes how a story came about is more interesting than the story itself.

So, does the Loch Ness monster really exist? Personally, I doubt it. But there is a whole world of creatures for you to explore. Some are only imaginary. Others vanished long ago. But they all have one thing in common—they are fantastic!

Andrew Whitmore has been writing ever since he could hold a pen. Science fiction and fantasy stories are his favorites. He has written two novels and loves to read.

Introduction

Nobody has ever seen a dragon, but everyone knows what they look like. In fact, some of the most famous animals in the world cannot be found in any zoo. Is there really a monster living in Scotland's Loch Ness? Do wild ape-men really roam the forests of North America, leaving over 15-inch footprints in the snow? Or are they just figments of the imagination?

Stories about weird and wonderful creatures are as old as humanity itself. Tales were told of birds big enough to carry elephants in their claws and giants the size of mountains. Glamorous mermaids, hairy ogres, and sea monsters amazed and scared people. The ancient world was a frightening place. It was easy for people to imagine monsters lurking just out of sight, just waiting to pounce on them.

No doubt a lot of the tales about such creatures were completely made up. People always like to swap scary stories around the

campfire.
Stories became
exaggerated
over the years,
with some based
on secondhand
reports of foreign
animals. Imagine what
the original white
settlers in Australia thought when
they first saw a kangaroo!

So what exactly are these fabulous
creatures that have fascinated people all over the
world? Is there a chance that any of them might
have existed? Or, deep down, do we just wish
they did?

Chapter 1: Introduction

Imagine . . .

listening to your grandfather telling old legends around a campfire.

"TELL US a story, Grandfather." Ina and her family squatted around the fire, plucking juicy pieces of baked fish from the coals.

"Yes, Grandfather," Rewa said. "Tell us a story about the old days."

Their grandfather laughed. He had fewer teeth than baby Muhu, and his face was as brown and wrinkled as dry seaweed.

"What kind of story?" he said.

"Tell us about the Giant with Teeth of Fire," Rewa said.

Ina nodded. Both she and Rewa had heard the tale many times, but it was still their favorite. And somehow their grandfather never told a story the same way twice.

"The Giant with Teeth of Fire, eh?" said Grandfather. "He was one mean fellow. Taller than ten palm trees. He was so heavy that the whole island shook whenever he stamped his foot."

"Ten palm trees, Grandfather?" Ina asked. She could have sworn it had been only eight last time he told the story.

"Oh, yes, little one. At the very least. And his teeth, they burned like coals of fire. His breath was very hot. It burned the leaves on trees for miles around every time he opened his mouth. And when he smiled—ah, it was terrifying to see, believe me. The glare of his burning teeth was brighter than the sun!

"He lived right up there in a big cave." Grandfather pointed at the dark mountain behind them. "Most of the time he just slept. And a good thing, too. Otherwise he would have burnt up the whole island. But, now and then, he would wake up and come striding down the mountain. Smoke and fire would pour from his mouth as he bared his terrible teeth. What a fearsome sight! All of the villagers would run and hide!

"Now some of the young men in the village had an idea. They thought how wonderful it would be if they could steal some of the giant's fire. No one knew how to make fire in those days, you see. People ate all of their food raw. They had nothing to keep them warm in the chill of the night.

"So, one day, the bravest and most daring of the young men got together. They gathered bundles of dried palm leaves. Then they quietly made their way up to the giant's cave.

"Luckily, the giant was fast asleep. With every breath, tongues of flame bubbled out through his huge lips, lighting up the cave.

"The brave young men crept closer and closer. If the giant woke up, they would all be killed. At last, they were close enough to poke the dried leaves into the flames around the giant's mouth. They waited for the leaves to catch fire, and then quickly turned and raced away.

"And that," Grandfather said with a smile, "is why we now have delicious feasts like this." He glanced at the piece of fish he was holding. Then he opened his mouth and popped it in.

"But that's not the end," Rewa protested. "Tell us the rest. You know, how the giant wakes up and chases them down the mountain. And how they hide in a cave. And—"

Grandfather laughed. "Ah," he said, turning toward Rewa with a gleam in his eye. "That's another story. . . ."

Chapter 1
Tall Stories

NO ONE KNOWS who made up the story of the Giant with Teeth of Fire. It has been told and retold for many generations throughout the Fiji islands. Perhaps it was based on half-forgotten memories of volcanic eruptions. What better way to explain the smoke and flames shooting out of a volcano? It made sense to blame it on some fire-breathing giant. And what else could possibly cause the very ground to shake except a giant's mighty footsteps?

But there has to be more to it than that. Stories about giants are told throughout the whole world. According to legend, they were so common in England that a boy named Jack spent half his life killing them. Ancient Jewish writings tell of giants who were two miles tall. There are Greek giants and African giants. Two Central American giants liked to pile up mountains, then knock them down with earthquakes. The Maoris of New Zealand like to tell how their country was formed. They say it was pulled up from the bottom of the sea by a giant fisherman.

eruptions: Lava exploding from the top of a volcano.

In fact, no matter where or when people lived, they all shared one common belief. They believed in the existence of giants at some time or another.

The only question is why?

Real-Life Giants

Statue of Robert Wadlow

There really are giants, of course. You've probably seen them on television hundreds of times. You might even have met some of them in person, or gotten their autograph. Perhaps you will even grow up to be one yourself.

Technically, any male human over 6 feet 6 inches (2 meters) tall is classified as a giant. The same is true for women over 6 feet 1 inch in height. That makes many of the best basketball players giants.

The tallest human being whose height we can be certain of was Robert Wadlow. Born in Illinois in 1918, he grew to be almost 9 feet tall and weighed over 440 pounds. As far as anyone knows, however, he didn't have burning teeth—and neither does Shaquille O'Neal. Nor would they be able to wade knee-deep in the ocean like the way the legendary King Og did.

Legendary giants—the kind you read about—aren't simply a bit taller than the average person. They are absolutely huge! But the odds of you ever seeing one of them are pretty slim. There is no evidence that creatures like this ever existed. Also, according to the laws of science, they cannot exist.

Too Big to Be True?

An average human being stands about 5 feet 8 inches (173 cm) tall and weighs around 132 pounds (60 kg). For someone to be double that size, they would have to weigh four times as much. Double that again, and their weight would be 16 times greater. Someone as tall as a two-story building would weigh as much as an elephant!

This is physically impossible. Even bodies the size of Robert Wadlow's have difficulty working properly. Wadlow could only walk with the aid of a stick. He had to wear braces on his ankles to stop them from collapsing under his own weight. It was hard for his heart to pump blood easily through his body. Because of this, he had virtually no feeling in his feet.

In fact, this was what killed him. One of the braces wasn't fitted properly. But Wadlow didn't notice anything until his skin became badly blistered. An infection set in, and he quickly died of blood poisoning. He was only 22 years old.

Giants of Old

If it's impossible for giants to exist, why is it that so many people thought that they did?

One reason is that people living long ago looked at the world much differently than we do. Most of us now believe that science and technology are constantly improving. If you're buying a car, for example, you'd probably choose the most recent model you could afford. The same goes for computers and just about everything else you can imagine. We expect that most things will just keep on getting better in the future as technology improves.

virtually: Almost entirely or very nearly close to.

In the past, however, people often thought the exact opposite. As far as they were concerned, everything was just getting worse and worse.

They imagined that their ancestors were a lot stronger, braver, and smarter than they were. This may seem strange to us, but they had good reasons for thinking that way. For one thing, it was very often true.

Dreams of a Golden Age

Throughout history, civilizations have come and gone. Some were wiped out by natural disasters, torn apart by civil war, or overrun by enemies. The period that followed the destruction was often a "Dark Age" of ignorance and poverty. Apart from confusing stories handed down from one generation to the next, these civilizations were forgotten.

Not all of them, however, vanished without a trace. Many left behind ruined cities and temples. These were often built on such a large scale that people assumed they were the cities of giants. Imagine how a person from the desert in Egypt felt when he saw the Great Pyramid. Or what he thought about the 65-foot (20-meter) statues of the pharaoh Rameses II.

These ancestors appeared to be superior in every way. Didn't it stand to reason that they must have been bigger, too?

Giant Builders

In the past, giants' creations seemed to be everywhere. Ancient Greeks believed that one-eyed giants, called cyclops, built the fortresses they found. Great stone circles found throughout Britain and Ireland were once thought to be the work of giants. The most famous stone circle, Stonehenge, is known locally as The Giant's Dance.

It wasn't just buildings and monuments that people believed were the work of giants. They thought that giants created many other things, too.

The Giant's Causeway in Northern Ireland was said to be the remains of a gigantic roadway built by giants. It was believed that this road had once stretched all the way to Scotland. But it was actually formed by a volcanic eruption. However, the 40,000 or so mostly six-sided rocks do not look natural. That is why people were fooled into believing that giants must have built them.

petrified: Something that has been turned into stone.

Some parts of the landscape were actually thought to be giants—or what was left of them anyway. According to Greek mythology, the Atlas Mountains in Africa were the petrified remains of a giant. This giant's job had been to hold the earth and sky apart.

Giant Bones

Further proof that giants existed came from the monstrous skeletons that kept turning up. We now know that these were actually the fossils of prehistoric animals like mammoths and cave bears. But back then, no one knew anything about these creatures. So it isn't surprising that they were mistaken for giants and other fabulous creatures.

On the Mediterranean island of Sicily, huge skulls were found with a single hole just under the forehead. These skulls were thought to be the remains of gigantic one-eyed men. They helped give rise to the legend of the cyclops. In fact, they were elephant skulls. The single hole was where the blood vessels and air passages ran down into the elephant's trunk.

It wasn't just the ancient Greeks who were fooled by large bones. Supposedly a French surgeon made this mistake when he examined bones found around the 17th century. He declared them to be the skeleton of a giant. He claimed the giant

mammoths: Large, hairy elephants that died out in the last Ice Age.

had shoulders over eight feet wide and eyes as big as dinner plates. Two hundred years later, they were identified as belonging to an early species of elephant.

If the bones obviously weren't human, they were usually attributed to dragons. People in Austria were sure their discovery in the 16th century was that of a giant dragon skull. They even built a large statue of a dragon in their town square to mark the occasion. But they were wrong. In fact, the skull was that of a woolly rhinoceros.

Larger than Life?

People throughout history have always loved to tell a good story. Like fishermen describing "the one that got away," ancient storytellers often made exaggerated claims about people.

The story of David and Goliath wouldn't be nearly as exciting if they were roughly the same size. We all love to see an underdog winning against the odds. Was Goliath really over nine feet tall? Probably not, but describing him that way certainly makes David's

species: A specific group of living things that share common characteristics.

victory seem even more remarkable.

Later generations often exaggerated the size of their heroes as well. Charlemagne, who united the tribes in France and became their first king, was without doubt a remarkable man. At the time of his death in 814 A.D., he ruled most of western Europe. He was probably big and strong, as kings had to be in those days. But there's no reason to believe that he was over seven feet tall. Nor that he was able to bend three horseshoes in his hands at once, the way legends claimed. But because he was so powerful in other ways, people thought he must have been huge as well.

Stretching the Truth

Not all stories concerning giants were meant to be taken seriously. The tales told about a gigantic lumberjack named Paul Bunyan are a good example.

Even as a young boy, Paul was incredibly big. Every time he sneezed, he blew the roofs off of the neighbors' houses. When he jumped into the water at the beach, he made a huge splash. It would flood the land for miles around.

Paul grew up to become the greatest lumberjack who had ever lived. He chopped down trees so quickly that his ax grew red-hot. Where other loggers kept dogs as pets, he had a giant blue ox called Babe. One summer, a twisty road prevented him from harvesting a particular group of trees. So Paul attached Babe to one end of the road and pulled it straight!

Of course, none of the people who told stories about Paul Bunyan believed he actually existed. If someone that big was wandering around the United States in the past, he would hardly go unnoticed. Storytellers were just having a bit of fun. And the more exaggerated the stories were, the more their listeners enjoyed them.

Perhaps some of the tales about legendary giants of the past happened in the same way.

No doubt there were people the size of basketball players in the past. There were probably even some as tall as Robert Wadlow. But there were no giants with teeth of fire. Nor were there 65-foot-high monsters like the one whose bones were reportedly dug up during the Roman Empire.

Human beings simply can't grow that big—except in people's imaginations.

Chapter 2: Introduction

Imagine . . .

finding a spooky, old diary in the attic.

"Hey," Hilary said. "Look at this."
After picking her way through a mess of boxes
and suitcases, Cheryl eventually found her
sister. She was hunched over a large, battered
trunk. It had been raining all weekend. They
had decided now was a perfect time to explore
the attic. So far, all they found were clothes
and some old newspapers.

"What is it?" Cheryl asked.

Hilary held up a dusty, leather-bound book.
"I don't know," she said, slowly flicking
through the pages. "Seems to be some kind of
old diary. Kind of hard to read though. Must
be very old by the look of it. I wonder . . ."
Suddenly her grip on the book tightened.
"Hey!" she said. "Listen to this!"

The creature is getting bolder. Last night I could hear it slithering around near the cellar door. I'm too afraid to go down there anymore, even in daylight. I have nailed the door shut as best I can. I just hope it is strong enough to keep the thing from escaping.

Cheryl laughed. "Nice try, Hilary," she said. "But the old 'thing in the cellar' routine is a bit lame, don't you think?"

"I'm not making this up," Hilary told her. "Honest! Take a look for yourself if you don't believe me."

Cheryl grabbed the book and scanned the page her sister had been reading.

Hilary was right about the handwriting. It was so jerky Cheryl could barely recognize some of the words. But she realized that Hilary was telling the truth.

"Wow!" she said. "Sounds just like one of those horror stories, doesn't it? Although I guess it was probably only rats."

"More like a snake," Hilary said. "It slithered, remember? See if there's any more about it later on."

Most of the remaining pages were almost completely unreadable. Something seemed to have been spilled over them and smeared the ink. One bit Cheryl could make out said the police . . . *found nothing during their investigations. They are apparently of the opinion that I am the victim of a repeating nightmare. They advised me to drink a cup of hot milk each evening before going to bed!*

Only the very last pages were undamaged. The writing here was even more untidy, as if it had been scribbled in a hurry. As Cheryl read it, she felt her skin crawl.

My candle is burning low. Soon I will be in darkness. And then the beast will come.

It is outside now: waiting, lurking. I can hear it slapping against the door like a bundle of wet rope. The lock can't hold much longer. My blood runs cold to think what will be revealed when the door opens.

I should have fled when I had the chance. Now it is too late. I will die here, devoured by an evil monster no one other than myself ever believed existed.

The door is starting to splinter! Something is pushing its way inside! Snaking toward me! Searching. Hunting.

Oh, no! It . . .

"Keep going," Hilary said in a hushed voice. "What happened next?"

"That's all there is," Cheryl told her. "The writing just trails off. Almost as if . . ."

26

Hilary's face was as white as a sheet. "As if what?" she whispered.

"Well, as if something grabbed his arm." Cheryl glanced nervously over her shoulder. Suddenly it seemed awfully quiet and lonely in the attic. "You know, before he could finish the sentence." . . .

Chapter 2

How to Build a Monster

A LOT OF HORROR stories end this way. That's because it's very hard to picture what a monster might actually look like. Even famous horror writers like H. P. Lovecraft had trouble inventing truly frightening monsters. One critic complained that Lovecraft's monsters always turned out to be some kind of invisible, whistling octopus.

If you were asked to draw a monster, what would it look like? It would be difficult to imagine something that doesn't look in some way like an existing creature. Many people would probably borrow pieces from the scariest animals they could find and put them all together. It might have the head of a snake, teeth like a shark, and the body of a giant spider. Or it might have six eyes and long blue arms, or tentacles, like an octopus.

Storytellers wanted to invent horrifying monsters. So they tended to mix parts from the scariest creatures they knew.

How Ugly Can You Get?

Monsters don't come much worse than the Gorgons. In Greek legends, these hideous women had snakes for hair, bulging eyes, and bronze claws. Just to top it off, their skin was covered with scales. They were so horrible that anyone who looked at them was turned to stone. The hero Perseus solved this problem. He used his polished shield

Medusa, a Gorgon

as a mirror so that he only saw their reflection. This way he was able to cut the head off one of them. Then he used the head as a weapon against his enemies.

Harpies wouldn't have won too many beauty contests, either. They had the body of a bird and the head and shoulders of a wrinkled, half-starved woman. As well as being unpleasant to look at, they were also described as extremely dirty and smelly.

Mix and Match

Taking part of one animal and sticking it on another has always been a popular way of creating monsters. The ancient Greeks did it all the time.

29

A basilisk

Griffins had the head of an eagle and the body of a lion. (Some, known as hippogriffs, had wings thrown in for good measure.) Both of these animals were regarded as extremely fierce and powerful. A combination of the two was even more scary. They were so big that they could carry off a pair of horses in their claws.

If you wanted something even more unusual, you simply kept adding bits and pieces. The basilisk, for example, had a rooster's head, bat wings, and the tail of a snake. Although not all that big, it was certainly a nasty piece of work. It could kill with a single glance from its red eyes.

The chimaera was stranger still. It looked like a lion with a goat's head growing out of the middle of its back. It also had a snake for a tail. It was so odd that the name, chimaera, is now often used to describe something that can't possibly exist.

The Human Angle

Sometimes the scariest monsters are those that look something like ourselves.

A giant snake would be very frightening. But we'd feel more afraid of one that was human from the waist up. That's what the ancient Greeks imagined that Echidna, the mother of all monsters, looked like.

A Centaur

Many legendary creatures combine human and animal characteristics. Centaurs had the head and chest of a man and the body of a horse. Satyrs and fauns were part human and part goat.

The sphinx had a woman's head, the body of a lion, and the wings of a bird. One of her favorite hobbies was asking people a riddle, then eating anyone who didn't know the answer.

Perhaps the oddest creature of all was the manticore. It combined the head of a man, the body of a lion, and the tail of a scorpion. It could shoot out poisonous spines. And it had three sets of razor-sharp teeth in its mouth. No wonder an ancient Roman writer described it as "the most noxious animal that ever infested the earth!"

noxious:
Harmful to your health.

A Hundred Heads Are Better than One

A great recipe for creating monsters is to add extra arms and legs—or even heads. The Greeks were good at that. Among Echidna's many offspring was a three-headed dog named Cerberus who guarded the gates of hell. Another of Echidna's sons, Geryon, had three heads and three bodies as well.

Having three heads was nothing compared to Echidna's husband, Typhon. With 100 heads, he made everyone else in the family seem almost normal!

One hundred was a popular number among Greek monsters. There were hundred-handed giants, who fought against the gods. A watchman named Argus had a hundred eyes. When he was killed, the queen of the gods took his eyes. She put them in the tail of the peacock.

Animal or Vegetable?

Some imaginary creatures aren't so much frightening as downright weird—the Lamb of

Tartary, for example. It looked like an ordinary sheep. But its wool was a lot softer and could be woven into cloth as smooth as silk. The big difference was that it supposedly grew on trees!

Well, not trees exactly. But such creatures did grow from seeds. Once planted, these seeds quickly sprouted into stalks about three feet high. The fruit produced on these plants was exactly the same size and shape as a real lamb. The lambs remained attached to the stalk all their lives, feeding on nearby grass. When they had eaten everything within their reach, they just shrunk and died.

Understandably, the farmers were extremely fond of the "Vegetable Lambs." They were good to eat, and they didn't need any care!

In Scotland, there are similar legends about something called the "Tree Goose." This tree produced large green fruit. When the fruit was ripe, it fell into the sea and out hatched a little pink goose.

Strangely, any fruit that fell on the land didn't produce any geese at all. But according to the local people, it was extremely tasty!

stalks: The main stems that support small plants.

Making It Big in Hollywood

Monsters are just as popular today as they were thousands of years ago. They appear in an endless number of novels, short stories, comic books, and video games. Images of them are constantly stomping, slithering, or oozing across our movie screens and television sets. But they aren't really much different from those invented by the Greeks.

A lot of monsters are simply scaled-up versions of everyday creatures. We've had giant ants, giant snakes, giant spiders, giant sharks, giant octopuses—even giant killer tomatoes! Perhaps the most famous film monster of them all, King Kong, is really just a big ape. Of course, you wouldn't want to call him that to his face. Not when he's big enough to climb the Empire State Building like a coconut tree to destroy planes.

Godzilla can breathe fire and shoot lightning bolts from his eyes. But when you get right down to it, he's nothing more than an oversized lizard.

Personally, my favorite movie monster is Gamera. He was a turtle the size of a skyscraper, and he starred in several Japanese science-fiction films. Whenever he needed to make a quick getaway, Gamera would pull his legs inside his shell. Then he'd blast off like a rocket. Whoever thought that one up certainly had a pretty wild imagination!

Out of This World

Monsters have to come from somewhere. For the ancient Greeks it was usually far-off countries like India and Africa. Nowadays people visit these places all of the time, so we need a new home for our monsters. Where better than outer space?

H. G. Wells was one of the first writers to use this idea. He had martians invade the earth in his famous novel *The War of the Worlds*. But his martians looked a lot like Lovecraft's invisible, whistling octopus.

Edgar Rice Burroughs invented a whole range of colorful creatures for stories like *A Princess of Mars*. Most have an extra pair of arms—except the hero's girlfriend. For some reason, she looks exactly like a beautiful Earth-woman. I suppose four-armed Martians may be fun to fight, but you wouldn't want to marry one!

Like other monsters, most space creatures are either mixtures of animals or part man and part beast. Those in the *Alien* series of movies look like a cross between insects and reptiles. They were scary enough to give anyone nightmares. The *Star Wars* movies feature everything from giant toads to elephant-headed drummers in a band.

Do-It-Yourself Monsters

Believe it or not, you might actually own a pet monster one day. The modern science of genetic engineering can already create living things never before seen in nature.

So far, this has mainly been done with plants. Scientists recently developed a blue rose by combining genes from another flower with those of a rose. You might wonder why they bother. After all, a blue rose isn't particularly useful. But it is different—and people around the world will pay good money to buy

genetic engineering: Changing the genes in the cells of plants and animals to create new types of living things.

something no one else has seen.

The same techniques may one day be applied to animals as well. Chances are that these creatures could look like a fabulous beast that we have only dreamed about. Imagine walking into a pet shop to buy a unicorn just as easily as you might buy a puppy!

In theory, human beings could even be modified this way. They could be given wings or claws like a lion. Perhaps they may even be given lots of tentacles if that is what was wanted.

Let's just hope things don't ever go quite that far. Having a unicorn for a pet is one thing. But someone being able to serve food to eight people at the same time is something else.

Here, There, and Everywhere

When you think about it, there are probably more monsters around nowadays than ever before. They are in books, movies, and on television. Some are remarkably similar to creatures described in ancient myths and legends. Others combine bits and pieces from just about every animal, vegetable, and mineral you can think of.

Each monster must have some parts that resemble animals or things we already know. If they didn't, we would be unable to tell that they are monsters.

So if something ever does crawl up out of your cellar, don't be surprised if it seems familiar. Unless, of course, it happens to be an invisible, whistling octopus. In that case, you might even not know it's there. Then a tentacle reaches out and grabs you just as you're about to finish your last senten . . .

Chapter 3: Introduction

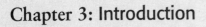

Imagine . . .

spotting a strange creature out in the middle of the sea.

WILL BUNDLED his winter jacket more tightly around him. It was bitterly cold on deck. But he was tired of cleaning dishes and scrubbing pots. When the cook wanted someone to take warm cider to the lookouts, he jumped at the chance.

Now he was beginning to think it might not have been such a good idea. The icy wind stung his face. His feet were already starting to go numb. He wondered how Tom and the others could stay up here so long without being frozen solid. He quickly walked across the deck.

Tom was keeping watch at the bow, so Will visited him first.

"Thanks, lad," Tom said. He gulped down a few mouthfuls of steaming cider and smacked his lips loudly. "Ah! Warms the heart, that does." He ruffled Will's hair. "So tell me," he said. "How are you enjoying life at sea? Still reckon you did the right thing signing on?"

Will shrugged. "It's not exactly what I thought it would be," he admitted.

"Oh, yes?" Tom said. "Why's that?"

"Well, I figured it would be a bit more exciting." Will looked out across the water that just seemed to go on and on forever. "Not much to look at, is there?"

Tom laughed. "You never know," he said. "The oceans are full of wonders, lad. Keep your eyes peeled. There's no telling what you'll see."

Will couldn't imagine what. The only remarkable thing about the voyage so far was how many times he'd been seasick.

"Might even spot a sea monster," Tom told

him. "I hear they're pretty common in these waters."

"Really?" Will looked at the sea more closely, trying to peer beneath the surface. "Ever seen one yourself, Tom?"

Tom shook his head. "But a man I worked with a few years back knew someone who had. Great ugly beast. Two hundred feet long and as wide as a lighthouse. Would have pulled the whole ship down if they hadn't scared it off with a cannon."

Will shivered. "Hey, what's that?"

Tom turned to look. "What's what?" he asked.

"Over there," Will said. He pointed to a dark shape bobbing up and down in the water nearby. "Looks like someone swimming."

"Nah," Tom told him. "It's too cold for that. You wouldn't last five minutes." He squinted, shading his eyes with one hand against the setting sun. Then he laughed. "Well, blow me down," he muttered. "It's a mermaid, lad! No mistake about it!"

"A mermaid?" Will peered more closely. The light was failing, so he couldn't see too clearly. But he supposed the shape did look a bit like that of a woman from the waist up.

"Hey, boys!" Tom shouted. "Come and look at this!"

One of the other lookouts rushed across to join them. The shape had drifted closer now. Will could see its soft, brown eyes gazing up at them and the wide smile on its face.

His heart thudded in his chest. It had to be a mermaid. Who else could live way out here, so far from land?

"Get a net!" Tom said. "We'll bring her aboard!"

Almost as he spoke, however, a sudden wave washed over her. Will glimpsed a sleek, forked tail going down through the water, then she was gone.

"Damn!" Tom said. "There's folks in London who'd pay a fortune for her!" He slapped Will on the back. "Ah well, lad, at least you'll have something to tell your grandchildren, eh?"

Will stared dreamily out across the empty sea. Yes, he thought. Yes, I will.

Perhaps a sailor's life wasn't going to be so boring after all. . . .

Chapter 3
Mistaken Identity

OFF THE COAST of Russia in 1608, a sailor named Thomas Hilles sighted a mermaid in the freezing water. His captain, Henry Hudson, recorded the sighting in his logbook. He described the mermaid as human-sized, with long black hair hanging down her back. She had a tail like a porpoise that was "speckled like a mackerel."

Tales of mermaids are as old as mankind itself. Even in recent times, people report seeing them everywhere, from Norway to the islands of the Pacific Ocean. Most of these stories are almost certainly made up. Other witnesses, like the two sailors on Hudson's ship, seem to have been telling the truth. At least they thought it was the truth.

Obviously Thomas Hilles and his fellow crewmate, Robert Rayner, saw something in the water that evening. Henry Hudson was one of the most famous explorers of his time. He wouldn't bother mentioning the incident if he thought his men had simply been pulling his leg.

> speckled: Marked with uneven spots or blotches.

Is it possible they actually did see a mermaid? If not, why were they so convinced that they had?

From Fantasy to Fake

Stories about creatures that were half human and half animal were common in ancient times. It was often a way to explain the forces of nature. A sea-god, for example, might have the tail of a fish. A sky-god might have wings like a bird. That's probably how legends about mermaids and mermen first started. But it doesn't explain why they have continued for so long.

If mermaids did exist, we'd certainly know about it. Either somebody would have photographed one, or their bones would have washed up on the shore somewhere.

Plenty of phony mermaids have been put on display over the years. The most famous of these was the "Feejee Mermaid." It earned the American showman P. T. Barnum thousands of dollars when he exhibited it in 1842. It was less than three feet long. It didn't even slightly resemble what most people imagined a mermaid to look like. This isn't really surprising.

The Feejee Mermaid

It was the top half of a small monkey sewn onto the bottom half of a fish.

At the time, creating fake mermaids was big business among Japanese fishermen. Supposedly one was sold in London for more than $40,000 during the 1830s. It's hard to imagine how anyone could believe that these tiny, dried-up bodies were real mermaids.

Do Mermaids Really Have Whiskers?

A manatee

Most likely, what many sailors mistook for mermaids were actually sea mammals. These may have included the manatee or dugong.

Both of these creatures are only slightly larger than human beings. Their bodies narrow from the waist down to a flat, flipper-like tail. The dugong often feeds its young with the top half of its body sticking up out of the water. Many sightings of "mermaids" describe them as doing exactly the same thing. If disturbed, these animals will dive beneath the surface, often flicking their tail in the air. This is just the way many "mermaids" are described when spotted in the water.

Of course neither dugongs nor manatees are particularly pretty. Christopher Columbus first saw some in 1492. He noted that "They are not as beautiful as they are painted." And no wonder. They have bulging eyes, squashed noses, and whiskers. They certainly don't look much like the beautiful women of myth and legend.

From a distance, female manatees might well look human. At least human enough for sailors to imagine that they were actually women with long, flowing hair.

Serpent or Squid?

Stories about sea monsters are almost as common as those involving mermaids. Although details vary, these monsters generally take one of two forms. Some resemble gigantic serpents, like the one seen from the ship *Daedalus* on August 6, 1848. In his report of the incident, the captain described the creature as being over 65 feet (20 meters) long. It had a large, snake-like head. And it had "something like a mane of a horse" hanging down its back. Other monsters, including the legendary

> serpent: A monster, sometimes snake-like, that usually lives in water.

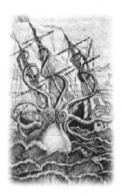

The kraken

kraken, have tentacles like an octopus. These tentacles are big enough to wrap around an entire ship and pull it under the sea.

Strangely enough, both kinds of monsters may be based on the same real animal. Giant deep-sea squid have long, tube-shaped bodies. They also have a beaked mouth surrounded by ten snake-like tentacles. Very few of these creatures have ever been seen. This is because they spend most of their time at the bottom of the ocean. Squid up to 55 feet (17 meters) long have been washed up on beaches. But they could possibly grow far larger than that. None of the bodies found so far have been fully developed. The world's foremost expert on giant squid estimates their maximum size could be about 150 feet!

A giant squid on the surface with its tail showing could easily be mistaken for a huge serpent. Eight of its tentacles are quite thin and might look a bit like hair. This would explain why so many sea serpents are described as having a shaggy mane.

foremost:
Highest ranked
or most famous.

We know that the giant squid sometimes attacks boats. In the late 1800s, some fishermen off the coast of Newfoundland were attacked. Thinking the squid was a piece of a ship, they tried to pull it toward them. The squid rammed them and threw a tentacle around the boat. If

A 1570 map showing sea monsters

12-year-old Tom Piccot hadn't cut off the tentacle with an ax, they could have been hurt or killed.

This 20-foot-long (6-meter) tentacle was the first solid evidence that giant squids actually existed. Up until then, all scientists had to go on were a few rotted remains found on the beach. Sometimes bits and pieces were found in the bellies of dead sperm whales. Giant squid apparently make up a large part of the sperm whales' diet. Imagine a battle between a 40-ton whale and a squid with tentacles 35 feet long!

Fact versus Fiction

One reason why people long ago readily believed in nonexistent animals is that hardly anyone ever

 traveled. Most people never went more than a mile from the village where they were born. As a result, they could only imagine what the rest of the world was like. To them, mermaids and unicorns were simply two creatures they had never seen—just like giraffes or elephants.

During the Middle Ages, everything known about the world's animals was collected in books known as bestiaries. The writers of bestiary books made no attempt to find out whether these creatures actually existed. Even the information they provided about real animals was often a mixture of fact and fable.

According to some bestiaries, lion cubs were born dead. They stayed that way until their fathers breathed life into them. Swans supposedly sang beautifully just before they died. But most swans cannot sing at all. Both swans and storks were believed to take on human form when they migrated south for the winter.

Compared with these tales, horned horses and women with fish's tails wouldn't sound that strange at all!

How the Unicorn Got Its Horn

During the Middle Ages, many stories were told about legendary animals. These stories were taken from even older books written by the ancient Greeks and Romans. But these books often gave very little information, even about real animals. Medieval authors often used their imaginations to complete the picture.

The unicorn was first described by the Greeks around 400 B.C. It doesn't bear much resemblance to the creature listed in bestiaries. Called the "monoceros," it was an extremely strong animal shaped more like a bull than a horse. It lived in India and was so fierce that no one had ever managed to capture one. In fact, the only animal that dared attack it was the elephant.

Now, as it happens, there was a strong, fierce, one-horned creature living in India—the rhinoceros. Of course, the horn of the rhinoceros isn't long and slender like a unicorn's. Over the years, however, people changed the idea of a white, single-horned beast into something much more glamorous.

Perhaps they were also influenced by the stories they heard about the Arabian oryx. These animals have long, sharp horns that are very straight. If this animal was seen sideways, it could easily look like it had only one horn instead of two.

Medieval writers must have combined parts of the rhino and the oryx. That's how they came up with a horse-like beast with a single horn and magical powers. Strangely enough, though we know that unicorns are not real, that's still how we picture them today.

Heads or Hands?

It's hard to think of any living creature resembling the Hydra. This legendary Greek monster had nine heads. The middle one was immortal and could not be killed. Every time one of its heads was cut off, two more grew in its place. The famous hero Hercules finally destroyed the beast. He burned away eight of the heads and buried the immortal one under a large rock.

In the Vatican museum in Rome, there is a marble tablet showing Hercules fighting the Hydra. The Hydra looks very much like a large octopus. Eight of the heads, of course, are the tentacles surrounding its real or "immortal" head.

Octopuses are common in the waters around Greece. They can have tentacles up to five feet long. Such creatures could be extremely dangerous. The Hydra was no doubt based on stories of their occasional attacks on fishermen.

The octopus is also able to grow replacement tentacles if any are bitten off. This would explain the Hydra's legendary ability to grow new heads.

The Monster in the Maze

The older the stories are, the more confusing they can become. Greek mythology tells of a creature with the body of a man and the head of a bull. It lived in the middle of a huge labyrinth on the island of Crete. The Minotaur, as it was called, lived on human flesh. Seven young men and seven maidens, sent from the city of Athens, were fed to it each year. A hero named Theseus eventually killed the Minotaur.

labyrinth: A place like a maze full of hallways in a complex design.

A number of half-remembered facts about ancient Crete probably contributed to this legend. We now know that the Cretans sometimes sacrificed children to their gods. We also know that one of the most powerful gods was in the form of a bull.

That explains the bull-headed monster eating young Athenians. But what about the maze? In the Greek language, the word "labyrinth" means something like House of the Double-Ax. Excavations in Crete have unearthed huge palaces thousands of years old. The largest, a place called Knossos, had several hundred rooms. Some of them had carvings of double-bladed axes on the walls. So it's likely that the labyrinth in which the Minotaur lived was actually the palace of Knossos. This place must have seemed like a huge, baffling maze to any ancient Greeks who saw it.

Still Making the Same Mistakes?

People's eyes often play tricks on them. It's easy to be misled by what someone thinks they saw. Or to be convinced that a story passed down through several generations is true. No doubt that's how many tales about nonexistent creatures

baffling: Hard to understand or confusing.

started—and how they still start today.

Every year thousands of UFO sightings are reported around the world. In most, if not all, cases there is nothing that mysterious about these objects. They might be comets, airplane lights, or even balls of lightning. But many people remain convinced that what they saw are flying saucers from outer space.

Like mermaids and other legendary creatures, these aliens have taken on a life of their own. Eyewitness reports of encounters with them are published in books and newspapers. Countless films are made about them. Yet there is no proof at all that they actually exist.

In the end, of course, it doesn't make much difference. Aliens will always be real to people who believe in them—just the way mermaids were to earlier generations.

Chapter 4: Introduction

Imagine . . .

reading in the newspaper the headline: Big Foot Photo Snapped by Local Scouts!

Two MEMBERS of the 3rd Rapid River Scout Troop claim to have stumbled across the legendary Big Foot. The pair, Jack Carter, age 14, and Dwayne Richardson, 15, were camping at Rapid River National Park. They even have a photograph to prove it.

The encounter took place late Saturday afternoon. They discovered several large footprints beside a stream in the nearby woods. "They were twice the size of ours," Dwayne said. "At least a foot long and almost as wide. We thought they were bear tracks."

Dwayne and Jack found more footprints leading into the woods and decided to see where they went. They followed the tracks for about half a mile. Finally, they caught up with their owner in a small clearing.

"It was just standing there," Jack said, "eating berries from one of the trees. Dwayne took a photo before it saw us and ran off."

According to the boys, the creature resembled a giant ape covered in long, reddish-yellow hair. It was well over eight feet tall.

The International Society of Cryptozoology (an organization that investigates reports of unknown animals) was told of the sighting. The members intend to search the area as soon as possible. The group claimed similar creatures have been sighted many times. These have occurred mainly in the forests of northern California. "They can't all be false alarms," a spokesperson said. "Big Foot is obviously out there somewhere—and sooner or later we're going to find him."

Local park rangers don't agree.

BIG FOO

PID RIVER. Two boys
ndered away to inv
ng towards them
anaged

"I've been working here 20 years," Frank Kirby said. "If there were any ape-men about, I'd know about it. The boys probably saw a bear standing up on his hind legs and got a bit confused."

Experts from the Wildlife Department, who have examined both the footprints and Jack's photo, are equally suspicious. "The tracks are entirely consistent with those of an adult brown bear," Dr. Samuel Alderton said. "As for the photograph—well, the quality is poor. It could be just about anything. But large bears certainly are seen in the Rapid River area at this time of the year."

Jack and Dwayne remain convinced that the creature was none other than Big Foot himself.

"I know a bear when I see one," Dwayne said. "This was not a bear. It was something else."

The boys plan to continue camping out at the park in the future. They have no intention of trying to hunt down the creature by themselves.

"I feel kind of sorry for the poor guy," Jack said. "He seemed more scared of us than we were of him. I think he would like to be left alone."...

Chapter 4
Living Proof

THE LAST STORY is not true. But similar stories appear regularly in newspapers all over the world. And it isn't just hairy ape-men that people claim to see. Others report sighting giant, long-necked lake monsters or flying reptiles. Even stranger creatures have been reported, such as the Jersey Devil. It was described as having "a head like a collie and a face like a horse."

Unfortunately, like Dwayne and Jack, none of these eyewitnesses can back up their stories with any good evidence. We just have to take their word for it. Which is why most scientists believe the creatures they describe are just as imaginary as mermaids.

Cryptozoologists aren't so sure. "Crytpo" is an ancient Greek word meaning secret or hidden. Zoologists are people who study animals. So cryptozoologists study secret or hidden animals— ones that have not been proven to exist. They take these reported sightings seriously. And then try to figure out what people may have seen.

But if creatures like Big Foot really do exist, what on earth are they?

Survival Stories

Cryptozoologists believe that some animals that we thought died out millions of years ago might still exist.

A coelacanth

Monsters, like the one supposedly living in Scotland's Loch Ness, could be some kind of dinosaur. Hairy giants like Big Foot, and similar creatures sighted around the world, could belong to ancient species of apes. Of course, that's all a pretty big maybe. But perhaps the idea isn't quite as crazy as it sounds.

Crocodiles, sharks, and turtles all existed long before dinosaurs. They have survived into the present day more or less unchanged. There are also recent examples of creatures thought to be extinct suddenly turning up alive and well.

In 1938, South African fishermen reported catching a fish over six feet long. It was unlike any they'd ever seen before. Scientists were amazed to discover it was actually a coelacanth. Until then, everyone believed this fish had died out with the dinosaurs. Yet there it was, as large as life. And it looked

extinct: No longer existing on Earth.

exactly the way it did in fossils dating back 300 million years.

If the coelacanth is still around, then other ancient creatures might be as well. The question is, how could they have managed to go unnoticed for so long?

Ends of the Earth

One answer could be that they live in very remote places like mountains and jungles.

The world is not as fully explored as most people think. A lot of what we see on maps is based on photographs or pictures taken by satellites. They only show us major features like rivers and mountains. They can't tell us about the sort of creatures that might live there.

Large parts of Africa are covered in rain forest. This forest is very dense. You can fly right over it without ever seeing what is hidden beneath. Even something as large as an elephant could go completely unnoticed.

remote: Far away from anything or very secluded.

The same is true of the Amazon Basin in South America. One 20th-century explorer described this area as "a vast night of trees" covering 2.12 million square miles.

Other areas in South America are even harder to get into. In Venezuela, there are flat-topped mountains known as mesas. They are cut off from the rest of the world by very high cliffs between 2,500 and 8,400 feet high. Some mesas are more than 18 miles long. Most have never been properly explored. It wasn't until 1935 that the highest waterfall in the world was discovered on a mesa.

It's amazing to think that a 3,212-foot (980-meter) waterfall can go unnoticed for so long. Just imagine what unknown creatures might be living there.

The World Is Full of Surprises

There are certainly plenty of animals out there left to be discovered. Thousands of new ones are identified every year. Most of these are quite small, of course, like insects and worms. But much larger creatures also show up from time to time.

vast: Very large in size.

In 1976, a U.S. Navy research ship discovered an unknown type of shark near Hawaii. It was over ten feet (three meters) long and weighed 1,639 pounds (745 kg). Because of its huge mouth and floppy, rubbery lips, scientists nicknamed the creature "Megamouth." No one had ever seen one before because they apparently live in very deep water. They have no reason to come to the surface.

A new kind of whale was found as recently as 1991. Another has been sighted at least 24 times in the eastern Pacific Ocean. But no one has caught one yet.

Several large land animals have also been discovered in recent times. The jungles of Vietnam have produced at least five over the past few years. These include a barking deer and the spindlehorn. One scientist described the spindlehorn as a "kind of goat, but a little bit strange."

Legends Come to Life

Every zoo contains a list of animals that were either unknown or regarded as legends until recent times.

Europeans didn't believe it when they first heard about "terrible, hairy men" who lived in Africa.

They thought the local people were making things up. It wasn't until 1847 that two Americans finally proved that the creatures actually existed. They were, of course, gorillas which are the largest apes on the planet.

The world's largest lizard wasn't discovered until 1912. A pilot crash-landed his plane on the small island of Komodo, part of what is now Indonesia. He reported seeing ferocious 10-foot (3-meter) dragons while he was there. Naturally, nobody believed a word he said. Not long after, however, an expedition to the island returned with some of these dragons to back up his story.

They aren't actually dragons, of course, just very big lizards. But they are still powerful enough to kill adult deer and wild pigs.

It wasn't until 1869 that the giant panda was known outside of China. Until then, the cuddly black and white animal was thought to exist only in Chinese legends.

Discoveries like these give hope to those who still dream of tracking down other unknown animals one day.

Scotland's Shyest Star

Just about everyone has heard of the Loch Ness Monster. This mysterious creature has been spotted on and off for more than 1,400 years. The first reported sighting dates back to the 6th century.

Nessie, as it is called, has become a huge tourist attraction in recent times. There is an Official Loch Ness Monster Exhibition Center where you can see displays about the creature. The gift shop there sells T-shirts, postcards, and other items with Nessie pictures all over them. Outside there is an artificial pond where a large model of the monster swims around.

It isn't just tourists who look for Nessie in this Scottish lake. Scientists have used underwater radar and small submarines to probe the lake's secrets. But the lake is very large, over 20 miles long. We still have no idea whether a monster actually lives there or what this creature might actually be. But the search will certainly continue.

artificial: Not real but made by humans to look natural.

Last of the Dinosaurs?

Nessie may be the most famous lake monster, but she certainly isn't the only one. A similar creature has been reported in the waters of Cadboro Bay in Canada. It has been given the scientific name cadborosaurus. However most people call it "Caddy."

Actually, monsters have been spotted in more than 90 different lakes and rivers. Lake Okanagan in British Columbia has one named "Ogopogo." Lake Champlain's is known as "Champ." Others have been spotted in many other countries all over the world, including Ireland, Sweden, Turkey, and Russia.

All of these creatures are usually described as having long, snake-like necks, humped backs, and paddle-shaped flippers. They seem to vary in length from 33 to 66 feet (10 to 20 meters).

Cryptozoologists point out that creatures very similar to this description lived millions of years ago. During the age of the dinosaurs, they were called plesiosaurs and were air-breathing reptiles. They needed to stick their heads out of the water every so often to breathe. Nessie and her North American cousins are usually spotted doing exactly the same thing.

An Unsolved Mystery

Could plesiosaurs have survived in a few isolated lakes the way coelacanths have in the world's oceans?

Most scientists don't think so. There simply isn't enough food in a place like Loch Ness. Especially to feed anything weighing more than 600 pounds. Scientists believe that what people have seen is nothing more than a large fish or eel.

Nessie's supporters suggest that there may be underground waterways linking the lake to the sea. This would enable the monster to come and go as she liked.

Some people think Nessie might travel overland. In 1933, a couple claimed they had to stop their car while she crossed the road in front of them!

The mystery of Loch Ness will probably never be solved. The only way to prove that Nessie doesn't exist would be to completely drain the lake. Even then, it could be said that she just didn't happen to be there at the time.

One thing is certain. Thousands of people will continue to visit Loch Ness every year. Their only hope is to see this famous monster with their own eyes.

An African Dinosaur?

Mokele-Mbembe is one of the names given to a mysterious dinosaur-like creature in Africa. It has attracted a great deal of interest recently. Expeditions have been sent to look for the beast in the dense rain

forest, where it supposedly lives. But they have been unsuccessful. More expeditions are planned for the near future.

The rain forests of Africa certainly seem a far more likely place to find dinosaurs than cold lakes. Its hot, wet climate hasn't changed much for 60 million years or so. Many of the plants that grow there are almost identical to the ones ancient dinosaurs fed on. After all, crocodiles appeared in the region around the same time. And they're still going strong. Couldn't it be possible that at least one species of dinosaur survived in this area as well?

According to the Pygmies, who live in these forests, Mokele-Mbembe stays in swamps and rivers. They say it is about the size of an elephant with a snake-like neck and a long, powerful tail. It is very shy and stays away from villages.

The only past or present creatures that fit this description are the sauropod dinosaurs. That's why people are so excited about it.

Unfortunately, no one has been able to prove that the creature actually exists. Investigators have only found a few unidentified footprints in the area. Perhaps we'll never know for sure one way or the other. Like the Loch Ness Monster, however, the hunt for Mokele-Mbembe is bound to fascinate people for many years.

Riddles in the Snow

Eric Shipton never did succeed in becoming the first man to climb the world's highest mountain. But when he returned from Mt. Everest in 1951, he did become famous for a very different reason.

He brought back from the Himalayan mountains photographs of huge footprints. These photos were regarded as the first

sauropod dinosaurs: Any in a group of four-legged dinosaurs with a small head and a long neck and tail.

real proof that the legendary Yeti, or Abominable Snowman, actually existed.

The footprints Shipton found were the same shape as a man's but over 12 inches long. Other mountain climbers in this area have reported seeing similar tracks. The footprints are much longer and wider than human ones. They are also sunk much deeper into the snow than those made by a human.

This suggests that they were made by something several times heavier than a man. If they are those of a Yeti, the creature must stand at least eight feet tall. It also must weigh half a ton.

According to the people of Tibet, Abominable Snowmen are giant creatures who live in caves in the mountains. Their bodies are covered in thick coats of dark brown hair. They have oval-shaped heads and white, hairless faces a bit like that of a gorilla. This description is amazingly similar to that of other ape-men reported to exist elsewhere.

Big Foot & Company

Big Foot is extremely famous in the northwestern United States. In fact, one county in the area passed a law making it illegal to kill one. Yet there is no proof that anyone has ever actually seen one.

Australia has its Yowies. To the native Indian of British Columbia they are Sasquatch. In China they are called Yeren. The Nguoi Rung, or Wildman, is said to inhabit the mountains of Vietnam.

Cryptozoologists believe these may all be related to a species of primitive man-like ape. Judging by the size of their teeth and other remains, these creatures were giants. They must have been around ten feet (three meters) tall. They would have weighed twice as much as an adult male gorilla. Their footprints would probably have been exactly the same size as those of Big Foot or the Abominable Snowman.

The only problem is that this primitive ape supposedly died out 500,000 years ago. Most likely it was killed off by mankind's early ancestors, who were smaller but much more intelligent.

But who knows? Perhaps some still survive in remote parts of the world. If so, we will surely track them down sooner or later. Something almost as tall as a basketball hoop and as heavy as a small car can't hide forever!

The Photo That Fooled the World

One of the biggest problems cryptozoologists face is that not everyone tells the truth. In fact, on investigation, some famous reports of unknown animals have turned out to be fakes.

In 1934, an English doctor named R. Kenneth Wilson produced an interesting photograph. He claimed he took it while visiting Loch Ness. It clearly showed a long-necked animal swimming in the water. The Surgeon's Photograph, as it was called, made Nessie an international star. It seemed to prove that there was some kind of strange creature living in the lake.

We now know, however, that the whole thing was an elaborate hoax. It was dreamed up by a man named Marmaduke Arundel Wetherell.

Wetherell was sent to Loch Ness to investigate reports about a monster seen there.

> hoax: A trick or practical joke designed to fool people into believing something that isn't true.

When he couldn't find a monster, he decided to make his own. He made a plastic and wood model of a head and neck one foot long. He attached it to a toy submarine. Wetherell then took a picture of the model. Then he had Dr. Wilson send the photo to the newspaper. Wetherell reasoned that if the picture came from a doctor, it was more likely to be accepted as real.

The truth behind the Surgeon's Photograph remained a secret for 60 years. It was finally revealed by Wetherell's stepson shortly before he died in November 1993.

So the thousands of books and articles that explain exactly what the photograph shows are based on nothing. The model used is probably still lying somewhere in Loch Ness where Wetherell left it!

Fact or Fiction?

Many reports of unknown animals are probably just cases of mistaken identity. Others may be outright lies. But that still leaves a few that might actually have some truth to them. If they're not investigated, how would we ever know?

Perhaps one day you will come face to face with one of these legendary creatures yourself. Then at least you would know for sure that they really do exist!

The glyptodont, an extinct mammal

In the meantime, the only way to separate fact from fiction is by examining the evidence. Also it is important to try and keep as open a mind as possible.

As one cryptozoologist says, "We're not just wasting our time looking for new animals. There are still a number of mysteries out there. That's what makes it so fascinating."

Chapter 5: Introduction

Imagine . . .

*hunting for the first time a
large, dangerous animal.*

Maui had never been
this deep in the forest before. The
trees grew thicker and taller with
every step. Their emerald
green leaves almost blotted out
the sun.

It was the first time he was
allowed to join the hunt. Until
now, he always had to wait at
home. Only the warriors
went in search of the Great
Red Bird. He held his spear
tightly, trying to remember
everything his father had told him.

Te Kuru was big and strong.
It could kill with a single

76

blow. Maui had seen hunters with legs broken and bellies ripped open by its terrible claws.

Suddenly Maui's father held up his hand. Something was moving behind a thick clump of bushes up ahead. He motioned for the hunters to spread out. They obeyed silently, forming a long line to either side.

"There!" his father shouted.

The hunters broke into a run, shouting and banging their spears together.

Maui scrambled to keep up. He glimpsed a brightly colored head in the underbrush; then it disappeared. For a moment, he thought the giant bird had escaped. Then he saw it again, moving clumsily through the trees.

The hunters followed but at a safe distance. They needed to wait until they reached open ground before closing in for the kill. Then they would be able to surround the creature and attack it from all sides at once. Even the strongest warrior couldn't hope to bring down something as big as Te Kuru on his own.

They were in luck. The forest slowly began to thin out. Soon they were jogging through knee-high grass rather than picking their way through tightly packed trees. A river lay just ahead, cutting off the bird's retreat.

With nowhere to run, Te Kuru turned to face them. Stretched to its full height, it was at least twice as tall as Maui's father. It looked much heavier than anything the hunters had brought back in the past. Its long neck waved menacingly from side to side. It glared down at them with huge orange eyes.

Now came the dangerous part. Some of the hunters darted forward, jabbing at the bird with their spears. Quick as a flash, Te Kuru lashed out with one giant foot. A hunter fell, howling with pain.

Maui could see blood pouring from his face.

Everyone was shouting and screaming. A few spears had found their mark, but Te Kuru was still on its feet. It towered above the ring of hunters like a feathered giant surrounded by children.

Then Maui saw his chance. Te Kuru was supporting all its weight on one leg. It had just aimed another kick at a nearby hunter. Almost without thinking, Maui darted in and smashed his spear into its knee. There was a loud crack. Next thing he knew, Te Kuru fell to the ground as its leg buckled beneath it.

The other hunters quickly closed in for the kill. Te Kuru kicked and squawked as the spears struck home then fell silent.

The Great Red Bird was dead.

Maui joined the other hunters to cut up the mighty beast. Not a scrap of it would be wasted. Its feathers would decorate his father's new robe. Its bones would be turned into fishhooks. Its skull would make a fine bowl for his mother.

Best of all, their tribe would feast well that night—and for many nights to come.

Maui felt someone grab his shoulder. He looked up to see his father standing over him.

"I did it, father!" he said. "I brought down the Te Kuru with my spear!"

His father smiled. "I know. May it be the first of many."

Maui's heart swelled with pride. "Oh, it will be, Father," he said. "It will be.". . .

Chapter 5
Lost Worlds

THE MAORI PEOPLE arrived in New Zealand around the 11th century. They hunted the Great Red Bird, or moa as we call it, until it was completely wiped out. The dogs and rats that came with the Maori people didn't help either. They killed many young moas for food.

As well as being one of the tallest birds that ever lived, moas were also one of the strangest. They couldn't fly because they were much too big and heavy. But unlike other flightless birds, such as ostriches, they had no wings or tails. Nor did moas have fully-developed feathers. They just had thin, silky ones that looked almost like hair.

Its distant cousin, the kiwi, still lives in New Zealand today. Although only about the size of a chicken, kiwis, like moas, lack tails and have the same hair-like feathers. But no other bird in the world will ever be able to replace the large and powerful moa.

An Island Paradise

Imagine a place where all animals lived peacefully together. A place where there were no snakes, rats, crocodiles, lions, or tigers. Sounds like paradise, doesn't it?

That's exactly what New Zealand was like when the Maori people landed there over 900 years ago. It had been cut off from the rest of the world for millions of years. This isolation prevented mammals that were common everywhere else on Earth from reaching there.

Birds had New Zealand almost to themselves. With few enemies to fly away from, they slowly lost the use of their wings. Flying took a lot of energy. It was a lot easier for them to just walk wherever they wanted to go. Some birds, like the moa, grew to be enormous. Others developed very strange habits. One kind of parrot, the kakapo, stopped flying. But this parrot can climb trees very well.

Unfortunately, many of New Zealand's weird and wonderful animals have now disappeared. Europeans began settling the country in the early 1800s. At this time they brought more than 100 different kinds of birds and mammals with them. These included everything from deer, rabbits, and sheep to blackbirds and sparrows. Having been isolated for so long, native species were unable to compete with these new animals. The native birds and animals were either completely wiped out, or their populations were greatly decreased.

A kiwi

Even New Zealand's national symbol, the kiwi, is rarely sighted in the wild today. Less than a hundred kakapos still survive. And the moa, of course, is gone forever.

The Truth Behind a Legend?

What sort of bird lays an egg one foot (30 cm) long and 8 inches (20 cm) wide? That's what the director of the Paris zoo wanted to know. In 1850, he was sent three of these eggs from Madagascar, an island off Africa. He imagined something like an ostrich, only as tall as a two-story house. He named the creature *Aepyornis maximus*. It means the tallest of the high birds, even though he had never seen one before.

Legends, nevertheless, were told about a giant bird living on Madagascar. It was called the ruhk. Sinbad the Sailor supposedly saw one when he

The ruhk

was shipwrecked on the island. The ruhks were said to be so big that they could carry adult elephants in their claws.

The real elephant bird wasn't quite that large. It couldn't fly, either, so there isn't much chance of one ever having carried off an elephant. But it was certainly big enough. It weighed over 1,000 pounds.

Gone—But Not Forgotten

Unlike its relatives elsewhere in the world, Madagascar's elephant bird must have survived longer that most. At least long enough to inspire legends about the ruhk.

A few elephant birds may even have been alive in the 19th century. Local people at the time used their eggs as water containers. But they said that the eggs were "very, very rarely" found anymore. By that stage, probably only a handful, if any, birds were still alive.

So why did the elephant bird disappear? The local people never hunted it for food. But they did raid the nests for eggs. This fact, along with changes in the climate that dried up the swamps where it lived, probably caused the bird's extinction.

Whatever the reason, it was extinct before any European ever saw one. All that remains are a few skeletons, some enormous eggs, and the legend of a giant bird. A bird that could carry elephants!

The World's Weirdest Wildlife?

Australia is home to some of the strangest animals in the world. It wasn't isolated as long as New Zealand. So early types of mammals managed to reach there. However, these mammals weren't replaced by more advanced species as happened in most places.

When Europeans arrived in Australia, they couldn't believe their eyes. The animals they found were unlike anything they'd ever seen before. They had trouble even describing them. Early explorers reported seeing a large animal with the head of a deer and a long tail. It not only stood on its hind legs like a bird, but it could also hop like a frog. Imagine what people back in Europe must have pictured the animal to look like. No wonder they thought it couldn't exist.

The platypus

What the explorers saw, of course, were kangaroos. They were just one of the many odd creatures living in the new land.

Perhaps strangest of all was a weird little animal discovered in Australia in 1797. When its body was sent to England, scientists thought it must have been a fake, like the Feejee Mermaid. Surely someone had attached a duck's bill to the body of a small, furry mammal. They examined the body carefully. But they couldn't find any stitches. Apparently it was a real animal after all. Most of us today know it as the platypus.

Giants of an Ancient Race

If Europeans thought platypuses were strange, it's a good thing they didn't arrive thousands of years earlier. Back then, Australia's wildlife was even weirder.

It was a lot bigger, too. *Dromornis*, for example, was one of the largest birds ever to walk the earth. It stood over 11 feet tall and weighed over half a ton. You would have needed a large hammer to break open one of its eggs. The shells were more than one and a half inches thick!

Plenty of giant mammals lived there as well. Some kangaroos were almost twice the size they are now. And they weighed around 660 pounds.

Australia was much greener and wetter in those days, with plenty of food to eat. As the climate changed, life became more difficult for many animals. The first people, the Aborigines, arrived somewhere between 40,000 and 100,000 years ago. This may have sealed the animals' fate. Giant, lumbering creatures would be easy prey for hunters.

Fortunately, Australia is a big country. Although giant creatures are no longer alive, there are signs of those ancient mammals today. They live on in the kangaroos and countless other creatures that still delight us.

lumbering: Moving slowly because of size and weight.

Frozen in Time

Not all of the giants in the past have disappeared completely. At least one can still be seen, even though it has been extinct for thousands of years.

Imagine a shaggy-haired elephant with huge, curved tusks over 16 feet long. That's what mammoths looked like. Great herds of them once roamed the frozen plains of northern Europe during the last Ice Age.

Mammoths were well suited to that cold period of time. But they couldn't adapt when the climate began to warm up again. They gradually died out altogether. The arrival of primitive human hunters around 12,000 years ago probably didn't help them to survive, either.

snap-frozen: Frozen so quickly that the animal stays in good shape.

Some mammoths, however, were snap-frozen in the ice. Several dozen of these bodies have been discovered over the past few hundred years. Their bodies are perfectly preserved, just like food from your freezer.

When Dr. Otto F. Hertz discovered one in Russia in 1900, its meat was still fresh. He fed some to his sled dogs. And he even ate a piece himself!

A Legend Reborn?

When people found bodies of mammoths buried in the ice, they thought the animals had just died. Legends spread about giant rats or moles that live in burrows under the snow. They were struck dead the moment they reached the surface. These legendary beasts were known as mammantu, which is how the mammoth got its name originally.

In September 1999, a French explorer cut a whole mammoth from the ice in northern Russia. Rather than letting it defrost, he transported it by helicopter to some nearby caves. That way scientists are able to examine it closely before the body starts to rot.

In the future, mammoths may walk the earth once more. This would be done by making a clone. A clone is an exact copy of an animal grown from a single cell.

Sheep have already been cloned. But no one knows whether cloning can be done with an animal that has been frozen.

Dead as a Dodo

Dodos haven't been gone as long as many other extinct animals. But they are certainly gone forever.

Around 1600, dodos lived on the remote island of Mauritius, 1,240 miles east of Africa. Only about the size of a large turkey, they were far too heavy to fly. In fact, they were so fat they couldn't manage more than a slow waddle. They were often described as being very stupid. They didn't even try to run away from hunters. Actually, they were just very trusting. If you grew up on a remote island with no natural predators, you'd probably behave the same way.

When predators arrived on Mauritius in 1598, the dodos were completely defenseless. Portuguese and Dutch sailors killed thousands of the birds for their meat. Dogs and rats brought by the new settlers feasted on dodo eggs and the young chicks. Within a few years, the dodos became very rare. Visitors to the island had trouble finding them.

The last living dodo was seen in 1681. The next time anyone tried to look for one, there were none to be

predators:
Animals that live by hunting and eating other creatures.

found. By 1750, the people on the island had forgotten that the bird ever existed.

People in the rest of the world were shocked when they realized what had happened. None of the dodos brought back to Europe survived. There wasn't even a stuffed specimen in any museum.

Less than 100 years after its discovery, the dodo had completely vanished from the face of the earth.

How Many Others Will Follow?

Scientists estimate that more than a hundred different kinds of animals become extinct every day. Most disappear almost without anyone noticing. Usually they are insects and tiny sea animals that only a few experts know about. Species are dying out faster now than they have at any other time in the past 65 million years.

specimen: A thing that represents or shows what something was like.

They aren't being hunted to extinction like the dodo. They aren't the victims of a changing climate like the large mammoths. The problem is that there isn't enough room in the world for all of the animals anymore.

Six billion people take up a lot of space. Huge areas of land are constantly being cleared to make way for towns and cities. Even more land is being turned into farms to feed the world's increasing population. That means there is less and less wilderness for animals.

Organizations that protect wildlife are doing what they can to save endangered animals. But it may already be too late for many of them. Thousands of parks and other protected areas have been set up around the world. But these only make up three percent of the earth's total land area. Everywhere else, thousands of creatures are being driven to extinction at a frightening rate.

To our grandchildren, giant pandas, tigers, rhinoceroses, and many other animals found in zoos today may have disappeared forever.

And the world will be a much poorer place without them. The fact is, no matter how fantastic imaginary creatures may be, they aren't nearly as wonderful as the real thing.

Where to from Here?

You've just read legends and tales about giants, dragons, and other imaginary beasts. Some are inspired by reports of long-extinct creatures. Here are some ideas for learning more about fantastic creatures.

The Library

Some books you might enjoy include.
- *Bigfoot* by Julie S. Bach
- *Monster Hunting Today* by Daniel Cohen
- *Monsters, Dinosaurs, and Beasts* by Stuart Kallen
- *Science Looks at Mysterious Monsters* by Thomas G. Aylesworth

TV, Film, and Video

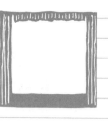

Watch TV listings for Public Broadcasting Station (PBS) programs and National Geographic specials about creatures such as Big Foot and Yeti. Check your video store for films about extinct creatures. Some suggestions are:
- *Walking with Dinosaurs*
- *Raising the Mammoth*

The Internet

Search the Internet using keywords such as *extinct animals, Loch Ness monster,* and *sasquatch.* A website to explore cryptozoology is *www.izoo.org/isc.*

People and Places

If there is a natural history or science museum nearby, visit and ask questions about extinct animals and species. Inquire about cryptozoology to find out more about the field.

The Ultimate Fiction Book

Be sure to check out *The Last Dinosaur,* the companion volume to *Fantastic Creatures. The Last Dinosaur* tells the story of a young girl's search in the jungles of central Africa for her missing father.

Decide for yourself where fact stops and fiction begins.

Index